INTRODUCTION

What are some of the weirdest sports you have heard of? How about extreme ironing or extreme sitting?

If you like reading random fun facts like these, you will like this 365 random fun facts for adults.

Impress your family and friends with these random facts and watch their faces go "WoW"!

GW00645540

1. Costa Coffee employs Gennaro Pelliccia as a coffee taster, who has had his tongue insured for £10 million.

2. Extreme ironing is a sport in which people take ironing boards to remote locations and iron items of clothing. It originated in England.

3. More tornadoes occur in the United Kingdom per square mile than any other country in the world.

4. You do not need cotton buds to clean a giraffe ears. It can do so with its own 50cm-tongue.

5. The Guinness World Record for the time longest spend searching for the Loch Ness Monster is held by Steve Feltham who camped at Loch Ness since 1991.

6. In 2009, Stephen Hawking held a reception for time travellers, but didn't publicize it until after. This way, only those who could time travel would be able to attend. Nobody else attended.

7. Tom Hanks had an asteroid named after him which was called "12818 tomhanks".

8. When Shakira was in second grade, she was rejected by the school choir because her vibrato was too strong. The music teacher told her that she sounded like a goat.

9. The first band to ever perform live on all seven continents was Metallica.

10. A Dutch start-up company has been able to start training wild crows so that they pick up cigarette butts and put them in bins for a peanut as a reward.

11. Before finally being accepted, J.K. Rowling's original Harry Potter pitch was rejected by 12 publishers.

12. It has been estimated that humans use only 10% of their brain.

13. The oldest unopened bottle of wine was found in a Roman tomb that is over 1,650 years old.

14. It's impossible to sneeze with your eyes open.

15. Polar bears often hunt walruses by simply charging at a group of them and eating the ones that were crushed or wounded in the mass panic to escape.

16. When the Titanic sank in 1912, there were 3 dogs that survived. They had all been traveling with their owners in the First Class cabins.

17. Coca-Cola was the first drink that was ever consumed in space.

18. Santa Claus was issued a pilot's license from the U.S. government in 1927. They also gave him airway maps and promised to keep the runway lights on.

19. Christmas was once illegal in England.

20. Will Smith owed $2.8 Million to the IRS and almost went bankrupt, just before he signed the contract for The Fresh Prince Of Bel-Air.

21. Even though Irish is the official language of Ireland, Polish is more widely spoken.

22. Researchers have found that Einstein's brain was 15% wider than normal.

23. Cruise ships are legally required to carry body bags and maintain a morgue.

24. Charlie Chaplin once won third prize in a Charlie Chaplin look-alike contest.

25. The motto on the United Kingdom's Royal Coat of Arms is in French. The motto is "Dieu et mon droit", which means "God and my right".

26. William Hung, made famous for his appearance on American Idol singing "She Bangs", is a 73rd generation descendant of Confucius.

27. One of Hitler's favorite tunes to whistle was the very popular, "Who's Afraid of the Big Bad Wolf?"

28. Octopuses only touch in situations of mating or aggression. Female octopuses sometimes do both, strangling and eating the male after mating.

29. Pope Francis used to be a nightclub bouncer.

30. A woman faked her entire tragedy and the loss of her husband during the 9/11 attacks and became President of the Support Network in New York.

31. Ben & Jerry's has an online flavor graveyard for their discontinued ice cream flavors. Each one has a photo, life span, and epitaph.

32. The British Pound is the world's oldest currency still in use at 1,200 years old.

33. The famous line in Titanic from Leonardo DiCaprio, "I'm king of the world!" was improvised.

34. Losing Weight is the most common New Year's resolution.

35. Mulan has the highest kill count of any Disney character, including villains, and was the first Disney Princess to be shown killing people on-screen.

36. In the 1980s, the founder of Pringles, Fredric Baur, requested to be buried in a Pringles can. His children honored the request.

37. While filming Rocky IV, Lundgren hit Sylvester Stallone for real and he ended up in the hospital.

38. In the popular film, The Godfather, the word "mafia" is never said because the actual mafia commanded it.

39. Ed Sheeran has a ketchup bottle tattooed on his arm.

40. The loudness of a monkey is relative to the size of its testicles. Researchers found that the smaller the testicles, the louder the monkey.

41. Celebrity chef Jamie Oliver has such severe dyslexia that he didn't read his first novel until he was 38.

42. In order to keep Nazis away, a Polish doctor faked a typhus outbreak. This strategy saved 8,000 people.

43. You're not allowed to swear if playing in Wimbledon. Because of this, line judges have to learn curse words in every language.

44. Herring fish communicate by using flatulence.

45. Thomas Edison, acclaimed inventor of the light bulb, was afraid of the dark.

46. A woman once tried to commit suicide by jumping off the Empire State Building. She jumped from the 86th floor but was blown back onto the 85th floor by a gust of wind.

47. Van Gogh only sold one painting when he was alive.

48. The Roman – Persian wars are the longest in history, lasting over 680 years. They began in 54 BC and ended in 628 AD.

49. Morihei Ueshiba, founder of Aikido, once pinned an opponent using only a single finger.

50. In ancient Egypt, priests plucked EVERY hair from their bodies, including their eyebrows and eyelashes.

51. The flea can jump 350 times its body length. It's like a human jumping the length of a football field.

52. The Guinness Book of Records holds the record for being the book most often stolen from public libraries.

53. Bruce Lee was so fast that they actually had to slow film down while shooting so you could see his moves. That's the opposite of the norm.

54. Ten percent of the Russian government's income comes from the sale of vodka.

55. Turkey vultures use defensive vomit to get rid of any disturbing animal. They can propel their vomit up to 10 feet.

56. A dog was the first living creature to be sent into space in 1957.

57. Women manage the money and pay the bills in 75% of all Americans households.

58. 65% of autistic kids are left-handed, and only 10% of people, in general, are left-handed.

59. The sperm of a mouse is actually longer than the sperm of an elephant.

60. In the marriage ceremony of the ancient Inca Indians of Peru, the couple was considered officially wed when they took off their sandals and handed them to each other.

61. 1912 saw the last Olympic gold medals made entirely out of gold.

62. The Black Widow spider eats her mate during or after sex.

63. If the population of China walked past you in single file, the line would never end because of the rate of reproduction.

64. Sudan has more pyramids than any country with 255. They outnumber Egyptian pyramids by twice the amount.

65. The king of hearts is the only king without a mustache.

66. A man with severe OCD and a phobia of germs attempted to commit suicide with a gun to his head. Instead of killing him, the bullet eliminated his mental illness without any other damage.

67. The electric chair was invented by a dentist.

68. Mosquito repellents don't repel. They hide you. The spray blocks the mosquito's sensors so they don't know you're there.

69. In 1933, Mickey Mouse, an animated cartoon character, received 800,000 fan letters.

70. Italy didn't have tomatoes and India didn't have peppers until the Americas were discovered.

71. Daniel Radcliffe was allergic to his Harry Potter glasses.

72. In Bruges, Belgium, there an underground pipeline that runs 2 miles to transfer beer from a brewery to the bottling plant.

73. The longest unbroken alliance in world history is between England and Portugal. It has lasted since 1386, and still stands today.

74. Peanuts can be used for a component to make Dynamite.

75. Albert Einstein and Charles Darwin both married their first cousins.

76. Dutch painter Vincent Van Gogh cut off his left ear. His Self-portrait with the Bandaged Ear shows the right one bandaged because he painted the mirror image.

77. Invented in 1923, Q-Tips were originally called Baby Gays; then Q-Tip Baby Gays, then finally just Q-Tips. The Q stands for quality.

78. If you put a raisin in a glass of champagne, it will keep floating to the top and sinking to the bottom.

79. Fingernails grow nearly 4 times faster than toenails.

80. There is a village in Russia called Tsovkra where every resident can tightrope walk. It is a tradition that dates back over 100 years but no one knows how it started.

81. Scotland was one of the few countries able to hold off being conquered by the Romans in the first century A.D.

82. Adolf Hitler's mother seriously considered having an abortion but was talked out of it by her doctor.

83. Originally, the Eiffel Tower was going to be erected in Barcelona, but the project was rejected because citizens thought it was an eyesore.

84. The average human will shed 18 kilograms of skin in a lifetime.

85. Steve Jobs named his company "Apple" partially because he wanted it to appear in the phone book before Atari, his former workplace.

86. Facebook is predominantly blue in color because Mark Zuckerberg is red-green colorblind and blue is the "richest color" that he can see.

87. From 1497 to 2016, the United Kingdom has printed their laws on vellum, made from calf or goat-skin.

88. Ants closely resemble human manners: When they wake, they stretch & appear to yawn in a human manner before taking up the tasks of the day.

89. Humans have been performing dentistry since 7000BC, which makes dentists one of the oldest professions.

90. Aeroflot Flight 593 crashed because the pilot let his kids fly the plane, who unknowingly disengaged the autopilot function.

91. Manatees can get frostbite in water below 20°C. Their fat is not designed to insulate them from the cold.

92. If your throat tickles, scratching your ear can make it go away.

93. In 18th Century England, having a pineapple was a symbol of wealth because of high import fees. They would be used as displays instead of being eaten.

94. Selfies now cause more deaths than shark attacks.

95. Part of the Falklands Islands is littered with leftover landmines from the Falklands War. It is now home to over 1 million penguins as they are too light to trigger the mine.

96. Erotomania is a psychological disorder where the sufferer has delusions that another person is in love with him or her.

97. Jack Daniel (the founder of the whiskey) died from kicking a safe.

98. Every time you lick a stamp, you consume 1/10 of a calorie.

99. Ladybugs bleed from their knees when threatened.

100. With the exception of a few organs, caterpillars liquefy almost completely while undergoing metamorphosis.

101. There is an island called "Just Enough Room", where there's just enough room for a tree and a house.

102. The last picture taken of John Lennon while he was alive had his killer in the frame.

103. In feudal Japan, lords purposely built homes with squeaky floors as a defensive measure against ninjas.

104. One of the earliest depictions of dreadlocks dates back to 1600 BC to the Minoan Civilization.

105. People can suffer from a psychological disorder called Boanthropy that makes them believe they are a cow.

106. During the Second World War, German tank drivers would drive their vehicles over camel droppings, thinking it would bring them good luck.

107. Marvel's Deadpool issue #27 holds the Guinness World Record for the most comic book characters on one cover.

108. Only primates, humans, and opossums have opposable thumbs. Out of these, the opossum is the only one with no thumbnail.

109. People who donate blood in Sweden are sent a text message each time their blood saves a life.

110. You can now get a headstone with a QR code. Called "Living Headstones", they show pages with photos, video biography's, and comments from loved ones.

111. The highest body count in film history goes to "Lord of the Rings: Return of the King" with 836 on-screen deaths.

112. Never get a camel angry, for he or she will spit at you.

113. Research indicates that mosquitos are attracted to people who have recently eaten bananas.

114. In almost every scene of Fight Club, there is a Starbucks coffee cup.

115. Italy built an entire courthouse to prosecute the Mafia. They charged 474 members in a trial that lasted from 1986-1992.

116. PewDiePie supported his YouTube channel by selling hot dogs before it garnered substantial subscribers.

117. Sweden has the most islands in the world, with 221,800 islands.

118. The most poisonous spider is the black widow. Its venom is more potent than a rattlesnake's.

119. It was once against the law to have a pet dog in a city in Iceland.

120. The first world leader to create a YouTube channel was the British Prime Minister, Tony Blair who made his account in 2007.

121. Prince Charles and Prince William never travel on the same airplane in case there is a crash.

122. Marie Antoinette's last words were to her executioner after accidentally stepping on his foot, saying, "Pardon me sir, I meant not to do it".

123. There was a snail glued to a specimen card in the British Museum mid-1800s. It spent four years glued there before scientists realized it was still alive.

124. The word "friends" is said in every episode of Friends.

125. Anatidaephobia is the fear that somewhere some how a duck is watching you.

126. Whenever Charles Dickens was away from home, he would always realign the bed he was sleeping in to face Northwards, as he felt that this fostered and unlocked his creativity.

127. It's Australian tradition to eat sausages at polling places on election day called Democracy Sausages.

128. In Japan, many families eat a KFC for Christmas Dinner. Many people order their meals months in advance and queue for hours to collect them.

129. Paddington Bear has 2 birthdays (just like the Queen).

130. It was Nicholas Cage who first advised Johnny Depp to pursue a career in acting, during the mid-1980s.

131. In space, astronauts are unable to cry, because there is no gravity and the tears won't flow.

132. In the Philippine jungle, the yo-yo was first used as a weapon.

133. The shortest war in history was between Zanzibar and England in 1896. Zanzibar surrendered after 38 minutes.

134. Women blink nearly twice as much as men.

135. Extreme sitting is a sport described as a cross between skateboarding and sitting down.

136. In 1778, fashionable women of Paris never went out in blustery weather without a lightning rod attached to their hats.

137. The longest recorded flight of a chicken is thirteen seconds.

138. When Nike first started, it was called Blue Ribbon Sports. The name was changed in 1971.

139. A person cannot taste food unless it is mixed with saliva

140. A Brussels airline flight to Vienna was aborted because the pilot was attacked in the cockpit. The attacker was a passenger's cat.

141. In World War II, Germany tried to collapse the British economy by dropping millions of counterfeit bills over London.

142. Scotland's national animal is the unicorn.

143. Einstein couldn't speak fluently until after his ninth birthday. His parents thought he was mentally retarded.

144. Chewing gum while peeling onions will keep you from crying.

145. Because metal was scarce, the Oscars given out during World War II were made of plaster.

146. The only domestic animal not mentioned in the Bible is the cat.

147. If one places a tiny amount of liquor on a scorpion, it will instantly go mad and sting itself to death..

148. William Shakespeare had a curse engraved on his tombstone to prevent anyone from moving his bones.

149. Elephants can die of a broken heart if their mate dies.

150. In eighteenth-century English gambling dens, there was an employee whose only job was to swallow the dice if there was a police raid.

151. For some time Frederic Chopin, the composer and pianist, wore a beard on only one side of his face, explaining: "It does not matter, my audience sees only my right side."

152. Eskimos have over 15 words for the English word of 'Snow'

153. Queen Elizabeth saved up post-war clothing ration coupons in order to pay for her wedding dress in 1947.

154. A shrimp's heart is in its head.

155. Certain frogs can be frozen solid then thawed, and continue living.

156. In Japan, watermelons are squared. It's easier to stack them that way.

157. Despite a population of over a billion, China has only about 200 family names.

158. When a Hawaiian woman wears a flower over her left ear, it means that she is not available.

159. Earthworms have 5 hearts.

160. Each king in a deck of playing cards represents a great king from history. Spades - King David, Clubs - Alexander the Great, Hearts - Charlemagne, and Diamonds - Julius Caesar.

161. The Bible, the world's best-selling book, is also the world's most shoplifted book.

162. More than 2,000 pounds of space dust and other space debris fall on the Earth every day.

163. During your lifetime, you will produce enough saliva to fill two swimming pools.

164. The world record for spitting a watermelon seed is 23 metres.

165. People say 'bless you' when you sneeze because your heart stops for a millisecond.

166. In 1859, 24 rabbits were released in Australia. Within six years the population grew to 2 million.

167. During it's lifetime an oyster changes its gender from male to female and back several times.

168. Shakespeare spelled his OWN name several different ways.

169. February 1865 is the only month in recorded history not to have a full moon.

170. The first meal on the moon was roast turkey, eaten by Neil Armstrong and Buzz Aldrin.

171. In downtown Lima, Peru, there is a large brass statue dedicated to Winnie-the-Pooh.

172. Alfred Hitchcock didn't have a belly button. It was eliminated when he was sewn up after surgery.

173. Leonardo da Vinci could write with one hand while drawing with the other.

174. A spider has transparent blood.

175. NBA superstar Michael Jordan was originally cut from his high school basketball team.

176. A man named Charles Osborne had the hiccups for 69 years.

177. Mel Blanc (the voice of Bugs Bunny) was allergic to carrots.

178. Back when dinosaurs existed, there used to be volcanoes that were erupting on the moon.

179. Walt Disney was afraid of mice.

180. Fictional/horror writer Stephen King sleeps with a nearby light on to calm his fear of the dark.

181. Pamela Anderson Lee is Canada's Centennial Baby, being the first baby born on the centennial anniversary of Canada's independence.

182. Most lipstick contains fish scales.

183. By applying even pressure on an egg, it is nearly impossible to break the shell by squeezing it.

184. Grapes explode when you put them in the microwave.

185. Canadians say "sorry" so much that a law was passed in 2009 declaring that an apology can't be used as evidence of admission to guilt.

186. On one slow news day on April 18, 1930, a BBC radio announcer blatantly said "there is no news".

187. In England, in the 1880's pants was considered a dirty word.

188. Feeding curry to a sheep reduces the amount of methane in its farts by up to 40%.

189. Human birth control pills work on gorillas.

190. When we think of Big Ben in London, we think of the clock. Actually, it's the bell.

191. If a horse wins a race "hands down" it means the jockey never raised his whip during the race.

192. There is a city in Norway called 'Hell'.

193. The color red doesn't really make bulls angry; they are color-blind.

194. The U.S. bought Alaska for 2 cents an acre from Russia.

195. The Lion King was originally called "King of the Jungle" before they realized that lions don't actually live in jungles.

196. Vatican City is the smallest country in the world, with a population of 1000 and just 0.2 square miles.

197. Ancient Roman surgeons were trained to block out the screams of human pain.

198. Margherita Pizza uses tomato, mozzarella, and basil toppings to represent the Italian national flag. It was originally to honor the Queen of Italy in 1890.

199. Antarctica is the only continent that turtles don't live on.

200. Woodpecker scalps, porpoise teeth, and giraffe tails have all been used as money.

201. The British government coined the slogan, "Keep Calm and Carry on" during World War 2 in order to motivate citizens to stay strong.

202. Vanilla flavoring is sometimes made with the urine of beavers.

203. Ireland has more redheads per capita than any other part of the world.

204. Of all the words in the English language, the word 'set' has the most definitions!

205. More people are afraid of open spaces (kenophobia) than of tight spaces (claustrophobia).

206. Standing around burns calories. On average, a 70 kilograms person burns 114 calories per hour while standing and doing nothing.

207. There is a Japanese village called Nagoro which has 35 inhabitants, but over 350 scarecrows.

208. Of the 70% of water covering the Earth only 3% of it is fresh, the other 97% of it is salted.

209. There is a hotel in Sweden built entirely out of ice; it is rebuilt every year.

210. A large flawless emerald is worth more than a similarly large flawless diamond.

211. Llamas can be used as guards against coyote attacks on sheep herds. Studies have proven that just one guard llama is an effective protector and can even kill the attacking coyotes.

212. The Hogwarts Express from the Harry Potter movies is a real train in Scotland.

213. In the Philippines, it is considered good luck if a coconut is cleanly split open without jagged edges.

214. In 'Silence of the Lambs', Hannibal Lector (Anthony Hopkins) never blinks.

215. When young, black sea basses are mostly female, but at the age of 5 years many switch sexes to male.

216. During WWII, a U.S. naval destroyer won a battle against a Japanese submarine by throwing potatoes at them. The Japanese thought they were grenades.

217. Billiards used to be so popular at one time that cigarette cards were issued featuring players.

218. Sprite was manufactured as Coca-Cola's response to the popularity of 7 Up.

219. It is forbidden for aircraft to fly over the Taj Mahal.

220. Butterflies have their skeletons on the outside of their bodies, this is known as the exoskeleton.

221. During the 1908 Olympics in London, the Russians showed up 12 days late due to the fact that they were using the Julian calendar instead of the Gregorian calendar.

222. A chameleon's tongue is twice the length of its body.

223. The Titanic was about three times bigger than Noah's Ark, with a volume of 4.6 million cubic feet.

224. In Brazil, Christmas is celebrated with fireworks.

225. The catfish has the most taste buds of all animals, having over 100,000 of them.

226. Liège, Belgium tried to use 37 cats to deliver mail in the 1870s. Most of the cats took up to a day to deliver the mail, and the service was short-lived.

227. Czechs are the biggest consumers of beer per male in the world.

228. When you exercise, the burned fat metabolizes to become carbon dioxide, water, and energy. Meaning: you exhale the fat that you lose.

229. Ketchup was sold in the 1830s as medicine.

230. IBM's motto is 'Think'. Apple later made their motto 'Think different'.

231. In bowling, three strikes in a row was called a turkey. The term originated in when at holiday time, the first member of a team to score three strikes in a row won a free turkey.

232. The founders of Google were willing to sell Google for $1 million to Excite in 1999, but Excite turned them down.

233. Every year 6,000 in the UK get hurt putting their trousers on.

234. In 1386, a pig in France was executed by public hanging for murder of a child.

235. The Leaning Tower of Piza is tilted because of the soft soil that it's built on – which has also protected it from at least 4 powerful earthquakes.

236. What is called a 'French kiss' in the English speaking world is known as an 'English kiss' in France.

237. The first movie ever to put out a motion-picture soundtrack was Snow White and the Seven Dwarves.

238. The postage stamps of Britain are the only stamps in the world not to bear the name of the country of origin.

239. The Chinese soft-shelled turtle urinates through its mouth.

240. Your stomach has to produce a new layer of mucus every 2 weeks otherwise it will digest itself.

241. Swedish meatballs originated from a recipe King Charles XII brought back from Turkey in the early 1800s.

242. "The quick brown fox jumps over the lazy dog" is an English-language pangram—a phrase that contains all of the letters of the alphabet.

243. When Joseph Gayetty invented toilet paper in 1857, he had his name printed on each sheet.

244. Iceland does not have a railway system.

245. The microwave was invented after a researcher walked by a radar tube and a chocolate bar melted in his pocket.

246. Cranberries are sorted for ripeness by bouncing them; a fully ripened cranberry can be dribbled like a basketball.

247. There is a company in Japan that has schools that teach you how to be funny. The first one opened in 1982.

248. In 2006, a Coca-Cola employee offered to sell Coca-Cola secrets to Pepsi. Pepsi responded by notifying the police.

249. Even when a snake has its eyes closed, it can still see through its eyelids.

250. The Bagheera kiplingi spider was discovered in the 1800s and is the only species of spider that has been classified as vegetarian.

251. A cockroach will live nine days without it's head, before it starves to death.

252. It takes more calories to eat a piece of celery than the celery has in it to begin with.

253. The word "gorilla" is derived from a Greek word meaning, "A tribe of hairy women."

254. Daniel Craig was an anonymous Storm Trooper in Star Wars: The Force Awakens.

255. IKEA is an acronym which stands for Ingvar Kamprad Elmtaryd Agunnaryd, which is the founder's name, farm where he grew up, and hometown.

256. You're born with 300 bones, but by the time you become an adult, you only have 206.

257. Shakespeare invented the words 'assassination' and 'bump.'

258. Johnny Cash took only three voice lessons before his teacher advised him to stop taking lessons and to never deviate from his natural voice.

259. While dinosaurs roamed the earth, they lived on every continent including Antarctica.

260. Norway has a 25-year statute of limitation on murder. This means if the murder happened more than 25 years ago, they cannot be charged.

261. More than 1,000 different languages are spoken on the continent of Africa.

262. Roselle, a guide dog, lead her blind owner down 78 flights of stairs during 9/11.

263. There's a bar in Yukon that serves a "Sourtoe cocktail". It consists of a shot of whisky with a human toe floating in the glass.

264. A crocodiles tongue is attached to the roof of its mouth.

265. Samsung means "three stars" in Korean. This was chosen by the founder because he wanted the company to be powerful and everlasting like stars in the sky.

266. Mona Lisa was stolen from the Louvre in 1911, which drew more visitors to see the empty space than the actual painting.

267. The largest Japanese population outside of Japan is in Brazil.

268. While shedding, geckos will eat their skin in order to prevent predators from finding and eating them more easily.

269. Lettuce is a member of the sunflower family.

270. In the Netherlands version of Sesame Street, instead of Big Bird, they have a bluebird named Pino. He was later established as Big Bird's cousin.

271. The lead singer of The Offspring started attending school to achieve a doctorate in molecular biology while still in the band.

272. The smallest thing ever photographed is the shadow of an atom.

273. Comets only reflect 4% of the light that falls on them, the rest is absorbed.

274. There is an insurance policy issued against alien abduction.

275. The unique smell of rain actually comes from plant oils, geosmin, and ozone.

276. The Great Wall of China is the only man-made structure visible from space.

277. Nutella was invented during WWII when an Italian pastry maker mixed hazelnuts into chocolate to extend his chocolate ration.

278. There is a company in the U.K. that offers "being hungover" as a valid reason for calling off work.

279. One of the smartest bird species is the magpie. They can even recognize themselves in mirrors.

280. Pope Francis has been given many extravagant gifts over the years, and one of them was a Harley-Davidson motorcycle.

281. If all the females in a group of clownfish die a male will change its gender in order to keep its group alive.

282. The tallest mountain in our solar system, Olympic Mons, is 3 times taller than Mount Everest.

283. In Switzerland, it is illegal to own just one guinea pig. This is because guinea pigs are social animals, and they are considered victims of abuse if they are alone.

284. There are over 12,000 known species of grass.

285. English is not native to the British Isles. It was brought to Britain in the mid 5th to 7th Centuries by German, Danish, and Dutch settlers.

286. Dinosaurs would swallow large rocks which stayed in their stomach to help churn and digest food.

287. Orlando Bloom has swinophobia, which is a fear of pigs!

288. The word 'MEME' was created by Richard Dawkins in 1976 essentialy meaning to imitate or pass on.

289. Eight of the ten largest statues in the world are of Buddha's.

290. There is a British chocolate scientist who insured her taste buds for £1 million.

291. Iceland was chosen as the training ground for Apollo astronauts because it was the most "moonlike" surface.

292. Mr. and Mrs. originated from using the words master and mistress.

293. Though most think it's Italian, pepperoni is an American invention. The first use of the word dates back to 1919.

294. Einstein's brain went missing when he died in 1955 and was lost for 23 years.

295. Daniel Radcliffe broke over 60 wands while filming the Harry Potter movies because he used them as drumsticks.

296. When Play-Doh was first developed in the 1930s, it wasn't a toy, it was a way to clean wallpaper.

297. Calling "shotgun" when riding in a car comes from the term "shotgun messenger".

298. Rabbits can be literally "scared to death" if approached by a predator when they are totally unaware.

299. Most dust particles in your house are made from dead skin.

300. The longest Cricket Test match lasted over 9 days between England and South Africa. It only ended because the English team would have missed their boat home.

301. Snakes can help predict earthquakes. They can sense a coming earthquake from 120 kilometres away, up to five days before it happens.

302. In general, people tend to read as much as 10% slower from a screen than from paper.

303. During World War II, the very first bomb dropped on Berlin by the Allies killed the only elephant in Berlin Zoo.

304. Nearly every brand of hard liquor is vegan.

305. There is an uninhabited island in the Bahamas known as Pig Beach, which is populated entirely by swimming pigs.

306. A water dropwort is a highly poisonous plant. If it kills you, it can cause you to smile after you die. This is called a sardonic grin.

307. If you travel across the Russia, you will cross seven time zones.

308. Jellyfish are considered biologically immortal. They don't age and will never die unless they are killed.

309. Makeup has been used by women since before Cleopatra's time.

310. In 1998, David Bowie released an internet provider called BowieNet. Subscribers were offered exclusive content and a BowieNet email. It was shut down in 2006.

311. The word "oxymoron" is itself an oxymoron. This is because it derives from Ancient Greek where "oxy" mean sharp and "moros" means stupid.

312. In California, you can get a ticket if you're driving too slow.

313. In Cambodia, rats are being trained to sniff out land mines. They can clear 200 square meters in less than 35 minutes, which usually takes 2-3 days with a de-miner.

314. Tutankhamun's parents were brother and sister.

315. Crows can remember the faces of individual humans. They can also hold a grudge.

316. All the paint on the Eiffel Tower weighs the same as ten elephants. It gets repainted every seven years without closing to the public.

317. The inventor of Vaseline, Robert Chesebrough, ate a spoonful of the stuff every single day.

318. God is the only Simpsons character who has five fingers. The rest of the characters are only seen with four.

319. Despite Mercury being the closest planet to the Sun, Venus is the warmest planet.

320. Britain's shortest river is the Brun which runs through Burnley in Lancashire.

321. Rick Astley has his own brand of beer. It was a collaboration between him and the Danish microbrewery Mikkeller; it's a red lager with "a hint of ginger".

322. Bob Marley's last words were "Money can't buy life".

323. In 2005, Frito-Lay launched Cheetos Lip Balm, but it was quickly taken off the market due to its failure.

324. When Jay-Z was 12, he shot his older brother in the shoulder for stealing his jewelry.

325. Arctic and Antarctic trace their names to the simple meanings of "Bears" and "Opposite the Bears".

326. Frederick Douglass was the most photographed man of the 19th Century. He wanted to ensure an accurate depiction of Black Americans during the Civil War.

327. Ketchup was originally a fish sauce originating in the orient.

328. Paul McCartney was only paid £1 for performing at the 2012 London Olympics Closing Ceremonies. He willingly donated his performance.

329. Karaoke means empty orchestra in Japanese.

330. In the 1830s, the ruler of Egypt Muhammad Ali Pasha wanted to disassemble the Giza Pyramids and use them as pre-cut building materials.

331. The females of some moth species lack wings, all they can do to move is crawl.

332. It is impossible to lick your elbow.

333. The call of a Kookaburra is used as the stock jungle sound effect in many movies and shows set in the jungles of Africa or South America, even though they are only in Australia and New Guinea.

334. Astronaut Neil Armstrong first stepped on the moon with his left foot.

335. Neptune was the first planet to be found through mathematical predictions rather than telescopic location.

336. If you went out into space, you would explode before you suffocated because there's no air pressure.

337. The cigarette lighter was invented before the match.

338. Any free-moving liquid in outer space will form itself into a sphere, because of its surface tension.

339. The glue on Israeli postage stamps is certified kosher.

340. Tug of War was an Olympic event between 1900 and 1920.

341. In 1980, a Las Vegas hospital suspended workers for betting on when patients would die.

342. The first product to have a bar code was Wrigley's gum.

343. Koalas never drink water. They get fluids from the eucalyptus leaves they eat.

344. A day on Venus is longer than a year on Venus.

345. The Dead Sea is roughly 8.6 times saltier than the ocean.

346. Goethe couldn't stand the sound of barking dogs and could only write if he had an apple rotting in the drawer of his desk.

347. Napoleon's penis was sold to an American Urologist.

348. Both U.S. and Soviet militaries have trained dolphins. They can be used for rescuing lost naval swimmers and locating underwater mines.

349. The pupils of a goat's eyes are square.

350. Paper was invented early in the second century by Chinese eunuch.

351. In the great fire of London in 1666 half of London was burnt down but only 6 people were injured.

352. The average person falls asleep in seven minutes.

353. The most common name in the world is Mohammed.

354. A pig's orgasm lasts 30 minutes.

355. A Pineapple is actually a bunch of small berries fused together into a single mass

356. It takes the insect-eating Venus Flytrap plant only half a second to shut its trap on its prey.

357. The shortest British monarch was Charles I, who was 4 feet 9 inches.

358. Some moths never eat anything as adults because they don't have mouths. They must live on the energy they stored as caterpillars.

359. Beethoven dipped his head in cold water before he composed.

360. Elvis had a twin brother named Garon, who died at birth, which is why Elvis middle name was Aron.

361. Australian soldiers used the song 'We're Off to See the Wizard' as a marching song in WWII.

362. Tigers have striped skin, not just striped fur.

363. The distance from your wrist to your elbow is the same length as your foot.

364. Banana trees are not actually trees – they are giant herbs.

365. Arabic numerals are not really Arabic; they were created in India.

Printed in Great Britain
by Amazon

14238783R00045